Workplace Struggles?

Don Barnes

Published by Don Barnes, 2024.

Table of Contents

About the Author

Don is the founder and author of Life Works in Threes!™ E-books. He is a lifelong Texan who has traveled extensively while taking a keen interest in human behavior. His curiosity about life and what drives humans led him to the discovery of how life works in threes. He coined this term as the *Tryune Concept*.

Don attended college on an athletic scholarship and then embarked on a 30-year career in the oil and gas industry. Since the year 2000, he has been a consultant for distributors and manufacturers of various industries. Along the way, he worked on his Tryune discovery in hopes of someday sharing his findings with those struggling unnecessarily... in life. What Don surmised from 40+ years of R&D was that people were struggling unnecessarily because they were not aware that "life works in threes." They, for the most part, have been living their lives by chance rather than by choice, he also discovered.

From this, he began focusing on the "mechanics of life" which shows formulas for success with subjects such as *life, health, money, purpose and so forth*. When people are able to grasp the Tryune Concept, they can apply the formulas with topics that interest them and begin eliminating the struggle. This epiphany is what triggered his Tryune venture and is now on the path of sharing with all who desire to improve on their lives.

Don currently resides in Southern California and Texas while overseeing his businesses and investments.

Life Works in Threes™

When I was a kid growing up, no one sat me down and said, "Okay Don, I'm going to show you how life works so that you can navigate your way through adulthood." I graduated from school, got married and went about my way with the "learn as you go" concept. It was kind of like putting together a backyard swing set without a set of instructions. Lots of frustration and do-overs, for sure!

My discovery of the "triune" word and noticing how things come together in threes is really what set me off on researching that maybe "life comes in three" ...sort of a mechanical approach to managing life, if you will. I combed the libraries and bookstores for information on this and found one book on the subject that was written back in 1951. The author's name was John S. Arant.

What Mr. Arant had to say is this "For lack of a better name, I have called this *The Triangle of Triumph* and therefore, consistent with the name, since most of these conclusions are built on the geometric figure of the triangle." He continued "All Life and all lives are seated in, and circumscribed by, the triangle. The Author and Source and Director of all life is Himself triune in character – Father, Son, and Holy Spirit. Man is of triple nature – body, mind, and spirit – and within those three there are many triangles – desires, development, decay; intellect, will, sensibilities. Of this "paced interlude in the midst of eternity" which we call time there is the triangle of Past, Present, and Future. Space – that limitless and measureless element of the physical universe – is best known in terms of Height, Breadth, and Depth. Try building yourself some triangles along the lines of your Will, your Work, your Way – You will find some interesting angles.

So, for the first time, I realized that life is designed in a mechanical way to come in threes. That means you don't have to rely on wishing and hoping things turn out okay. You can actually look at the three parts that a particular thing is made of and then apply them to get what you're wanting. Like a three-ingredient recipe or a combination lock. With a combination lock, you need the three exact numbers to unlock the lock...otherwise you will continue to struggle.

Some 40 years later, I accumulated things that work in threes and that's when I knew I needed to share this with anyone wanting answers. To have success/harmony in your life, just apply the three parts of an area you're working on, and things will fall into place. I also learned that the recipe for success with just about anything is by doing these three things, consistently – THINK positively, SPEAK positively and ACT positively. For example, if I want to be a successful artist. I would think to myself "I can do this because I have the talent." Then I would speak it this way "Yes, I am working on my art degree and plan to do portraits professionally." Finally, I would act on that by taking art classes and continue crafting my skill. Eventually, I will see the positive results/success I'm looking for.

Conversely, if I think positively but speak negatively...it will cancel out. Or if I speak positively but have no positive action going on...nothing will happen.

I looked up "How Life Works" and "The Mechanics of Life" and these are really talking about the biology of how our cells work and other chemistry. TRYUNE WORKS! teaches that life is kind of like building blocks. Pick a topic you may be struggling with. See the three parts that topic consists of and then start applying them...on a consistent basis. That will help you overcome the struggle and get you back in harmony/success with how life works.

For 30+ years I was a golf instructor (by accident). My two kids had some success playing junior golf and so friends and neighbors would ask me to show them and their kids how to play golf successfully. From all of this, I got pretty good at watching golfers on the driving range and could spot right away why they were struggling with hitting bad golf shots. I was able to do that because I knew the three steps to hitting good golf shots. I learned them from studying golf and played for several decades. I "broke the code" for me so to speak.

So now you know that life works in threes. You can live your life *by choice* rather than *by chance* and that my friend... is the key to a fulfilling life.

LIFE WORKS
IN THREES!

My sanctuary on the Pacific coast

Introduction

The workplace is a significant part of our lives, often consuming roughly a third of our waking hours. This substantial time commitment underscores the importance of creating a supportive and secure environment. When we think about the hours spent at work, it becomes clear that this setting is not just a place for professional tasks but also a key aspect of our daily lives and personal well-being. As such, our workplace should be more than just a venue for earning a living; it should be a space where we feel valued, respected, and safe.

A sense of safety at work is crucial for both mental and physical well-being. When employees feel secure, they are more likely to be engaged, productive, and satisfied with their roles. Safety in the workplace encompasses not only physical safety but also emotional and psychological security. A supportive environment where harassment, discrimination, and undue stress are actively addressed fosters a positive atmosphere. This safety enables individuals to focus on their work, innovate, and contribute effectively, enhancing both personal growth and organizational success.

Moreover, fostering a safe workplace has broader implications beyond individual well-being. It contributes to a culture of trust and mutual respect, which can significantly impact overall organizational health. When employees know that their concerns will be addressed and that they are working in a safe environment, it reduces turnover, boosts morale, and enhances team cohesion. Ultimately, investing in a secure and supportive workplace benefits everyone, creating a thriving environment where individuals and organizations can flourish together.

My discovery of the Tryune Concept

Before we dive into the workplace struggles and how to overcome them, let me share my discovery of the Tryune Concept and how life works in threes. It all began in the summer of 1982.

I grew up with parents who treated everyone with decency and respect. My three older sisters and I were raised in a home that was "middle-class traditional." We lived in modest homes in different small towns, attended school and church on a regular basis and celebrated all the traditional holidays. Eventually we settled during the spring of 1964 in the big city of Houston, Texas. I'll never forget the vastness of the city and hearing sirens from police cars, fire trucks and ambulances on a regular basis. I was excited and scared at the same time.

Once settled in this fast-paced city, I finished my growing-up years with an academic diploma and sweetheart intact. I got a job, bought a car, got married, bought a house and produced two beautiful babies in a span of about 5 years. Talk about having to grow up fast!

Things went from great in my childhood to absolute misery in my young adulthood. I began to struggle with my job because deep down I just hated what I was doing. This problem created a snowball effect because soon after, my weight, my finances, my relationships, my happiness and everything else worth saving was going down the drain. I eventually hit a level of frustration that I had never experienced before and didn't know how to get out of it. My cry for help was for anyone or anything to come to my rescue. I just ran out of solutions for my situation.

This is when my discovery happened.

One night shortly after my meltdown, while sleeping soundly, the word "triune" began to softly pound in my head like a mantra. I woke up a little startled and decided to go look up the word in my favorite dictionary (this was WAY before Google.) The definition said '**triune** (try-une) – 1) a group of three things; united. 2) Being 3 in 1 such as *humans are mental, physical and spiritual.* I scratched my head, got a glass of water and went back to bed.

The next day while driving around town, I began thinking about things that I was taught in my younger years that came in threes. My Boy Scout manual taught that to have **character**, I needed to be *1) physically strong, 2) mentally awake and 3) morally straight.* My high school football coach would say emphatically "If you want to be **a good football player**, you have to be *1) mobile 2) agile and 3) hostile!*" My first sales manager shared with me that to be **a successful salesman**, I needed to have *1) sales skills, 2) product knowledge and 3) a good image.*

"Hmm", I thought, "wonder if there are other examples out there of things that work in threes?" So, some 40 years later, I have researched and discovered that many, many things work in threes. What this message was telling me is that to achieve success or balance in any significant area of my life, the three things that area consisted of had to be present continuously. That's when I had my epiphany. This discovery was telling me the secret to how life <u>really</u> works.

Tryune is a play on the word "triune" as an invitation to "try" this concept. Furthermore, we do not say that life <u>only</u> works in threes. Life also works in ones, twos, fours and so on. What has been observed though is that the many things significant to life, just so happen to come and work in threes. That's what is being shared in this book.

Now, you are about to see 40+ years of research and proof that life works in threes. I did not make up any of these topics. I invite you to research them on the internet to validate what is written here. There are some interesting facts that most of us have never realized...until now.

How Life Works in Threes (around 200 examples)

<u>**LIFE**</u>

Humans consist of *body, mind and soul.*

A human's basic needs are *health, income and provisions.*

A human's basic wants are *comfort, gain and approval.*

Our minds are made up of the *conscious, the subconscious and the unconscious.*

Philosophy explains *the id, the ego and superego.*

Atoms consist of *protons, neutrons and electrons.*

Motion is explained by *three basic laws.*

Science falls under three main branches: *natural, social and formal sciences*

Time is *past, present and future...*at the same time.

Electricity consists of *ohms, amperes and voltage.*

Music's basic elements are *duration, pitch and timbre.*

Democracy is a government *of the people, by the people and for the people.*

U.S. branches of government are *the judicial, the executive and the legislative.*

Armed Forces protect us on *land, air and sea.*

Environmentally, we are asked *to reduce, recycle and re-use.*

The news program gives us *the news, sports and conditions.*

Our days consist of *morning, afternoon and evening.*

Three months in each season of the year

Our main meals are known as *breakfast, lunch and dinner.*

A balanced diet consists of *good proteins, carbohydrates and fats.*

Traditional Family consists of *father, mother, and child(ren)*

SCIENCES

Three major branches of natural science – *(physical, earth/space and life sciences)*

Three major branches of modern physics - *(classical, relativistic, quantum)*

Three major branches of biology *(botany, zoology, microbiology)*

Three spatial dimensions: *height* (up/down), *width* (left/right) and *depth* (forwards/backwards)

Three-gauge bosons (photon, gluon, W&Z bosons)

Three types of elementary particles *(leptons, quarks, gauge bosons)*

Three quarks in every proton (*two "up" and one "down"*)

Three primary colors of light (*red, green, blue*)

Three color tone properties (*hue, value, chroma*)

Three laws of motion (*Newton's laws*)

Three laws of planetary motion (*Kepler's laws*)

Three layers of the Sun's interior (*core, radiative zone, convective zone*)

Three layers of the Sun's atmosphere (*photosphere, chromosphere, corona*)

Three types of meteorites (*iron, stony iron, stony*)

Three types of galaxy shapes (*elliptical, spiral, irregular*)

Three substances of the universe (*normal matter, 'dark matter', 'dark energy'*)

Three phases of the moon (*new moon, first quarter, full moon*)

Three planetary regions (*temperate, sub-tropical, tropical*)

Three layers of the Earth (*crust, mantle, core*)

Three components of an ecosystem (*producers, consumers, decomposers*)

Three types of rocks (*igneous, sedimentary, metamorphic*)

Three types of fossil fuels (*coal, crude oil, natural gas*)

Three hydrological processes (*evaporation, condensation, precipitation*)

Three basic types of (meteorological) precipitation (*liquid, freezing, frozen)*

Three types of substances (*mono-constituent, multi-constituent, UVCB)*

Three phases of (normal) matter (*solid, liquid, gas*)

Three types of covalent chemical bonds (*single, double and triple bonds*)

Three isotopes of hydrogen (*protium, deuterium, tritium*)

Three atoms in each molecule of water (*two hydrogen atoms and an oxygen atom*)

Three endings to salts (*-ide, -ite, -ate*)

Three requirements for fire (*fuel, oxygen, heat*)

Three nucleotide bases in a genetic codon

Three domains of life (*archaea, bacteria and eukaryotes*)

Three major groups of flowering plants (*monocots, eudicots, magnolids)*

Three major functions that are basic to plant growth and development: (*photosynthesis* [making sugars], *respiration* [metabolizing those sugars], and *transpiration* [water vapor loss]

Three things that the chlorophyll in plants needs for photosynthesis to take place: *(sunlight, carbon dioxide and water)*

Transpiration serves three roles: *(cooling the plant, moving minerals* and *sugars through the plant,* and *maintaining the turgidity pressure* [stiffness] *of the plant's cells)*

Three parts of an insect's body *(head, thorax, abdomen)*

BIOLOGY

Three types of cones in the retina, relating to the three primary colors

Three semi-circular canals in the ear *(lateral, anterior, posterior)*

Three sections in the ear *(outer, middle, inner)*

Three ossicles in the middle ear *(malleus, incus, stapes)*

Three segments to each limb *(proximal, mid, distal)*

Three bones in each arm *(humerus, radius, ulna)*

Three joints in the arm *(shoulder, elbow, wrist)*

Three joints in the leg *(hip, knee, ankle)*

Three joints in the elbow *(humeroulnar, humeroradial, proximal radioulnar)*

Three functional compartments in the knee joint (*the femoropatellar, medial femorotibial* and *lateral femorotibial articulations*)

Three types of fibrous joints (*sutures, gomphoses, syndesmoses*)

Three types of bone in each hand (*carpals, metacarpals, phalanges*)

Three types of bone in each foot (*tarsals, metatarsals, phalanges*)

Three bones (phalanges) in each finger and in each toe (*proximal, intermediate, distal*)

Three layers of skin (*dermis, epidermis, hypodermis*)

Three components of a cell (*cell membrane, nucleus, cytoplasm*)

Three types of blood vessels (*arteries, veins, capillaries*)

Three types of blood cells [*red* (erythrocytes), *white* (leukocytes), *platelets* (thrombocytes)]

Three processes of the intestinal tract (*ingestion, digestion, excretion*)

Three germ layers (*Endoderm, Mesoderm, Ectoderm*)

Three parts of a human tooth (*crown, neck, root*)

Three organs of otolaryngology (*ear, nose, throat*)

Three major body systems *(digestive, circulatory, respiratory)*

Three parts to a neuron*: (soma [cell body], axon, dendrites)*

Three main parts of the brain *(forebrain, midbrain, hindbrain)*

Three parts of the forebrain *(cerebrum, thalamus, hypothalamus)*

Three parts of the midbrain *(colliculi, tegmentum, cerebral peduncles)*

Three parts of the hindbrain *(cerebellum, pons, medulla)*

Three membranes enclosing the brain *(dura mater, arachnoid, pia mater)*

The brain operates on three levels: *consciously* (for cognitive thought and declarative memory); *subconsciously* (for pre-planned actions and procedural memory); and *unconsciously* (for breathing, heart beating, etc.)

Our conscious mind is fed from three sources: *our senses* (which can be fooled); *our memory* (which is flawed); and *our imagination* (which is inventive)

Three aspects of the human mind *(memory, intellect, will)*

Three parts of the human personality *(id, ego, superego)*

The sum of human capacity consists of three abilities *(thought, word and deed)*

Three times of man *(birth, life, death)*

Three periods of the Gait Cycle *(initial double limb support, single limb support, and terminal double limb support)*

MUSIC

Three types of musical notes *(sharps, flats, naturals)*

Three aspects of a song *(lyrics, melody, rhythm)*

Three types of musical chords *(root, third, fifth)*

MATHEMATICS

Three types of a real number *(positive, negative, zero)*

Three parts to any arithmetic operation: for addition: *augend, addend and sum* - for subtraction: *minuend, subtrahend and difference* - for multiplication: *multiplicand, multiplier and product* - for division: *dividend, divisor and quotient*

Three laws of arithmetic operations *(commutative, associative, distributive)*

Three types of equivalence relation *(reflexivity, symmetry, transitivity)*

Three types of symmetry operations *(translation, rotation, reflection)*

Three geometries *(Euclidean, spherical, hyperbolic)*

The number 3 is the basis of an entire branch of mathematics, called trigonometry (from the Greek *trigonon* "triangle" + *metron* "measure")

Three trigonometric functions (*sine, cosine, tangent*)

Three types of average (*mean, mode, median*)

<u>GRAMMAR</u>

Three logical operators (*AND, OR and NOT*)

Three laws of logic (*identity, noncontradiction, excluded middle*)

Three parts of a logical syllogism (*major premise, minor premise, conclusion*)

Three grammatical parts to a sentence (*subject, verb, complement*)

Three persons in grammar [*1st person* (I/we), *2nd* (you or your), *3rd* (he/she/it/they)]

Three genders in grammar [*masculine* (he/him), *feminine* (she/her), *neuter* (it)]

Three forms of comparison in grammar [*positive, comparative* (more, -er), *superlative* (most, -est)]

Three cases in (English) grammar [*subjective/nominative* (he), *objective/accusative* (him) and *possessive/genitive* (his)]

Three parts of a narrative (*beginning, middle, end*)

Components of an essay (*introduction, body, conclusion*)

Elements of a rhetorical appeal (*ethos, pathos, logos*)

Aspects of a story *(plot, characters, setting)*

<u>**RELIGION**</u>

The Creator – *omniscient, omnipotent, omnipresent*

Christian God – *Father, Son, Holy Spirit*

Jesus – *The Way, The Truth, The Life*

Ancient Near East- *Qudshu, Astarte, Anat*

Classical Antiquity – Many dieties came in threes

Hinduism – Para Brahman is *Brahma, Visnu, Shiva*

Ancient Celtic Cultures – *many example of triad dieties*

Buddhism – *The three jewels*

Taoism – *The three pure ones*

Islam – *Fear, Hope and Love*

Baha'i - *Intention, Power and Action*

Confucianism – *Benevolence, Wisdom and Courage*

<u>**OTHER TRIUNE EXAMPLES**</u>

3 Coins in a Fountain

3 Days of the Condor

3 Miles in a League

3 Goals in a Hat Trick

3 Piece Suit

3 Feet in a Yard

3 Books in Lord of the Rings

3 Ring Circus

3 Ships of Christopher Columbus

3 Sheets to the Wind

3 Books in a Trilogy

3 Wheels on a Tricycle

3 Wise Men

3-Legged Race

3 Ring Circus

3-Wheeler

3 Cornered Hat

3 Dimensional

3 Musketeers

3 R's (reading, 'riting, 'rithmatic)

3 Sides of a triangle

3 Races in the Triple Crown (horse racing)

3 Angles in a Triangle

3 Trimesters in a Pregnancy

3 Flavors in Neapolitan Ice Cream

3 Stars in Orion's belt

3 Barleycorns in an Inch

3 Hands on a Clock (with the Seconds Hand)

3 Colors in a Flag

3 Minute Egg

3 Great Pyramids at Giza

3 Holes in a Bowling Ball

3 Colors in a Set of Traffic Lights

3 Minutes in a Boxing Round

3 Teaspoons in a Tablespoon

3 Legs on a Stool

3 Monastic Vows (Obience, Stability, Conversatio Morum)

3 Body Types: Endomorph, Mesomorph, Ectomorph

3 Ring Notebooks

3 Germ layers: Endoderm, Mesoderm, Ectoderm

3 Species of Homo: Homo habilis, Homo erectus, Homo sapiens

3 Basic parts of a camera: Lens, Shutter, Sensor

3 Stages of a Project lifecycle: initiation, planning, execution

The Truth, The Whole Truth and Nothing but the Truth

Life, Liberty and the Pursuit of Happiness

Hear no Evil, See no Evil, Speak no Evil

National motto of France/Haiti: Liberty, Equality, Fraternity

Paper, Rock, Scissors

Ready, Aim, Fire

On Your mark, Get Set, Go

Olympic medals of gold, silver, bronze

Types of joints (ball & socket, hinge, pivot)

Stages of a rocket launch (launch, orbit, re-entry)

Parts of a joke (setup, delivery, punchline)

Primary components of a transistor (emitter, base, collector)

Primary components of an airplane (fuselage, wings, empennage)

Basic components of a computer: CPU, memory, storage

Three phases in the development of technology (*eotechnic* [*mechanical*], *paleotechnic* [*steam-powered*] and *neotechnic* [*electric-powered*]

Communication systems require three components (*transmitter, channel, receiver*)

The list goes on. See if you can find more examples as they are everywhere in our universe! Now that you know that life works in threes (with proof!), we can begin to apply this concept to whatever topics we want.

So, to overcome struggles in the workplace, we need to apply the three areas that the workplace consists of – SAFETY, INCLUSION and WORK-LIFE BALANCE. Let's get started!

SAFETY
WORK PLACE
INCLUSION
WORK-LIFE BALANCE

WORKPLACE

To ensure that a workplace is a healthy place to work, three critical elements must be in place:

1. **Physical Safety and Health Measures**: A healthy workplace must prioritize physical safety by adhering to regulations and best practices for occupational health and safety. This includes maintaining clean and hazard-free environments, providing appropriate safety equipment, and ensuring that facilities are ergonomically designed to prevent injuries. Regular maintenance and risk assessments, along with emergency preparedness plans, are essential to safeguard employees from physical harm and ensure their well-being.

2. **Supportive and Inclusive Culture**: A positive and inclusive workplace culture is fundamental for employee well-being. This involves fostering a respectful and collaborative environment where diversity is celebrated, and discrimination or harassment is actively prevented and addressed. Support systems such as mentorship programs, regular feedback mechanisms, and employee assistance programs contribute to a culture where individuals feel valued, heard, and supported, which enhances overall job satisfaction and morale.

3. **Work-Life Balance and Flexibility**: To promote mental and emotional health, a workplace must support work-life balance and offer flexibility. This can be achieved through policies that accommodate personal needs, such as flexible working hours, remote work options, and adequate leave policies. Encouraging employees to take breaks, manage their workloads effectively, and maintain boundaries between work and personal life helps prevent burnout and supports long-term productivity and happiness.

The COVID-19 pandemic has dramatically transformed the workplace landscape, introducing changes that have redefined how we work and interact. One of the most significant shifts has been the widespread adoption of remote work. What was once a relatively rare arrangement has now become a mainstream practice for many organizations. The pandemic forced companies to quickly pivot to remote work models, revealing both the potential and challenges of working from home. This shift has led to a reevaluation of traditional office spaces, with many businesses now considering hybrid models that combine in-office and remote work, reflecting a newfound flexibility in how work is approached.

The pandemic has also accelerated the integration of digital tools and technologies. Virtual meetings, cloud-based collaboration platforms, and advanced communication tools have become essential for maintaining productivity and connectivity in a remote work environment. Organizations have had to invest in and adapt to these technologies rapidly, leading to a more tech-centric workplace. This shift has not only changed how tasks are completed but has also highlighted the importance of digital literacy and access to reliable technology, which are now critical for both employees and employers.

Moreover, the pandemic has heightened awareness of employee well-being and mental health. The isolation and stress associated with remote work, coupled with the blurring of work-life boundaries, have underscored the need for supportive mental health resources and practices. Companies are increasingly focusing on creating environments that promote mental wellness, such as offering virtual counseling services, implementing flexible work hours, and encouraging regular check-ins. This emphasis on mental health reflects a broader recognition of the importance of a holistic approach to employee well-being in today's transformed work environment.

Training
SAFETY
Equipment
Report/
Response

SAFETY

Ensuring employee safety in the workplace requires a strategic approach with a focus on practical and effective measures. Here are the top three safety measures that should be in place:

1. **Comprehensive Safety Training and Protocols**: Regular and thorough safety training is essential for equipping employees with the knowledge and skills needed to handle potential hazards. This training should cover emergency procedures, use of safety equipment, and protocols for handling specific risks related to their work environment. Regular refresher courses and drills help keep safety awareness high and ensure that employees are prepared to act effectively in case of an emergency. Clear and accessible documentation of safety protocols should be available to all employees.

2. **Effective Safety Equipment and Infrastructure**: Providing appropriate safety equipment and maintaining a safe physical environment are critical. This includes ensuring that all necessary personal protective equipment (PPE) is available and used correctly, as well as maintaining and regularly inspecting safety infrastructure such as fire alarms, emergency exits, first aid kits, and ventilation systems. Proper ergonomic adjustments and maintenance of equipment are also crucial to prevent injuries related to repetitive strain or unsafe working conditions.

3. **Robust Reporting and Response Systems**: A reliable system for reporting safety concerns and incidents is vital for maintaining a safe workplace. Employees should have clear channels to report hazards, near-misses, and accidents without fear of reprisal. Additionally, there should be a structured process for investigating these reports and implementing

corrective actions. Regular reviews and updates to safety practices based on feedback and incident analysis help to continually improve safety measures and address any emerging risks promptly.

Training
SAFETY
Equipment
Report/
Response

Training

Safety training and protocols are fundamental components of a secure and effective workplace. Comprehensive safety training equips employees with the knowledge and skills necessary to identify and manage potential hazards, ensuring that they are prepared to respond appropriately in various situations. This training should be thorough and cover a range of topics including emergency procedures, proper use of personal protective equipment (PPE), and specific safety practices relevant to their roles. Regular refresher courses are also essential to keep safety practices top of mind and ensure that employees are updated on any new protocols or changes in safety regulations.

In addition to initial training, clear and accessible safety protocols must be established and communicated throughout the organization. These protocols should include detailed instructions for responding to emergencies such as fires, chemical spills, or medical incidents. Employees should know the location of emergency exits, first aid kits, and fire extinguishers, as well as understand the procedures for evacuating the building or seeking help. It is crucial that these protocols are documented and readily available, with visible signage and regular reminders to reinforce their importance.

Effective safety training should include practical drills and exercises to test employees' preparedness and reinforce their learning. Conducting regular safety drills helps employees practice their response to emergency scenarios, making them more confident and capable in real situations. Additionally, a robust system for reporting safety concerns and incidents ensures that potential issues are addressed promptly and that improvements are made based on real feedback. By combining thorough training, clear protocols, and practical experience, organizations can create a safer work environment and promote a culture of safety and preparedness.

Training
SAFETY
Equipment
Report/
Response

Equipment

The workplace is a significant part of our lives, often consuming roughly a third of our waking hours. This substantial time commitment underscores the importance of creating a supportive and secure environment. When we think about the hours spent at work, it becomes clear that this setting is not just a place for professional tasks but also a key aspect of our daily lives and personal well-being. As such, our workplace should be more than just a venue for earning a living; it should be a space where we feel valued, respected, and safe.

A sense of safety at work is crucial for both mental and physical well-being. When employees feel secure, they are more likely to be engaged, productive, and satisfied with their roles. Safety in the workplace encompasses not only physical safety but also emotional and psychological security. A supportive environment where harassment, discrimination, and undue stress are actively addressed fosters a positive atmosphere. This safety enables individuals to focus on their work, innovate, and contribute effectively, enhancing both personal growth and organizational success.

Moreover, fostering a safe workplace has broader implications beyond individual well-being. It contributes to a culture of trust and mutual respect, which can significantly impact overall organizational health. When employees know that their concerns will be addressed and that they are working in a safe environment, it reduces turnover, boosts morale, and enhances team cohesion. Ultimately, investing in a secure and supportive workplace benefits everyone, creating a thriving environment where individuals and organizations can flourish together.

Training
SAFETY
Equipment
Report/
Response

Report/Response

Having a well-defined report and response protocol in place is crucial for maintaining a safe and responsive workplace. Such protocols provide employees with a clear and systematic way to report safety hazards, near-misses, and incidents, ensuring that potential issues are addressed promptly. This structured approach helps in identifying and mitigating risks before they escalate into serious problems. A well-communicated reporting system empowers employees to take an active role in workplace safety, fostering a culture of vigilance and accountability.

Effective response protocols are equally important as they outline the steps that should be taken once a safety issue is reported. This includes procedures for investigating incidents, implementing corrective actions, and communicating findings to relevant stakeholders. A robust response protocol ensures that safety concerns are not only reported but also thoroughly addressed, minimizing the risk of recurrence. By having a clear plan for how to handle various types of safety issues, organizations can ensure a swift and organized reaction, which is crucial in preventing injuries and maintaining operational continuity.

Furthermore, having a transparent report and response system builds trust and reinforces a culture of safety within the organization. Employees are more likely to engage with safety protocols when they know their concerns will be taken seriously and addressed effectively. This transparency also helps in identifying systemic issues and opportunities for improvement, leading to more informed decision-making and enhanced safety practices. Ultimately, a strong report and response protocol contributes to a safer, more efficient workplace where employees feel supported and confident in their safety measures.

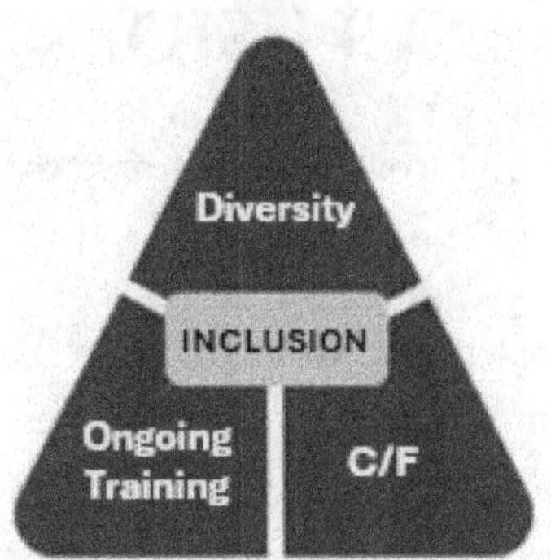
Diversity
INCLUSION
Ongoing
Training
C/F

INCLUSION

To cultivate an inclusive workplace culture, three key elements are essential:

1. **Diverse Representation and Inclusive Policies**: A truly inclusive culture starts with diverse representation at all levels of the organization. This involves not only hiring individuals from varied backgrounds but also ensuring that these employees are present in leadership and decision-making roles. Inclusive policies should be established to support this diversity, such as equitable hiring practices, anti-discrimination policies, and accessible career advancement opportunities. Implementing these policies ensures that all employees have equal opportunities to succeed and that the organization reflects a commitment to diversity in both its workforce and its leadership.

2. **Ongoing Education and Training**: Regular education and training on diversity, equity, and inclusion (DEI) are crucial for maintaining an inclusive culture. This training should cover topics such as unconscious bias, cultural competence, and effective communication strategies. It helps employees understand and address their own biases, recognize the value of diverse perspectives, and foster a respectful and inclusive environment. Additionally, providing resources and support for continuous learning and development in these areas reinforces the organization's commitment to creating an environment where everyone feels valued and respected.

3. **Open Communication and Feedback Mechanisms**: Establishing channels for open communication and feedback is vital for an inclusive workplace. Employees should feel comfortable sharing their experiences, concerns, and

suggestions regarding inclusivity without fear of retaliation. This can be facilitated through regular surveys, feedback sessions, and dedicated support systems such as diversity committees or resource groups. Actively listening to employee feedback and taking tangible actions based on their input helps to address issues and continuously improve the inclusivity of the workplace. By fostering an environment where communication is encouraged and valued, organizations can create a more responsive and supportive culture.

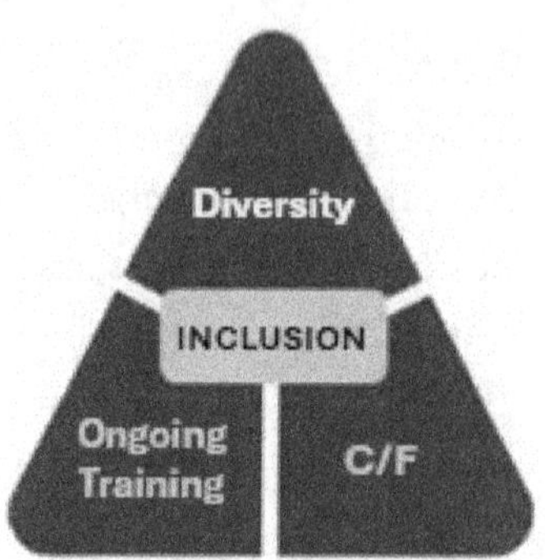
Diversity
INCLUSION
Ongoing
Training
C/F

Diversity

Diverse representation and inclusive policies are foundational to building a thriving and equitable workplace. When an organization reflects a broad range of perspectives and experiences, it enhances creativity, innovation, and problem-solving. Employees from varied backgrounds bring different viewpoints and approaches, which can lead to more effective solutions and drive the organization forward. Diverse teams are better equipped to understand and meet the needs of a diverse customer base, contributing to a competitive advantage in the marketplace. Moreover, when employees see themselves represented in leadership and key roles, it reinforces their belief in the organization's commitment to fairness and opportunity, leading to increased job satisfaction and retention.

Inclusive policies are equally critical, as they establish the framework for ensuring that all employees have equal access to opportunities and are treated with respect and fairness. These policies should encompass equitable hiring practices, anti-discrimination measures, and support for career development, among other areas. By implementing clear policies that promote inclusion, organizations can create an environment where all employees feel valued and empowered. This not only helps in preventing biases and discrimination but also fosters a culture of respect and collaboration, where diverse talents and perspectives can flourish.

Having robust diversity representation and inclusive policies enhances the organization's reputation and attractiveness to top talent. In today's competitive job market, prospective employees are increasingly prioritizing diversity and inclusion when choosing employers. Organizations that demonstrate a genuine commitment to these principles are more likely to attract and retain high-quality candidates who value an inclusive work environment. This commitment also contributes to a positive organizational culture and public image, showcasing the company as a leader in promoting equity and inclusion within the industry. Ultimately, diverse representation and inclusive policies are integral to creating a supportive and dynamic workplace that drives long-term success.

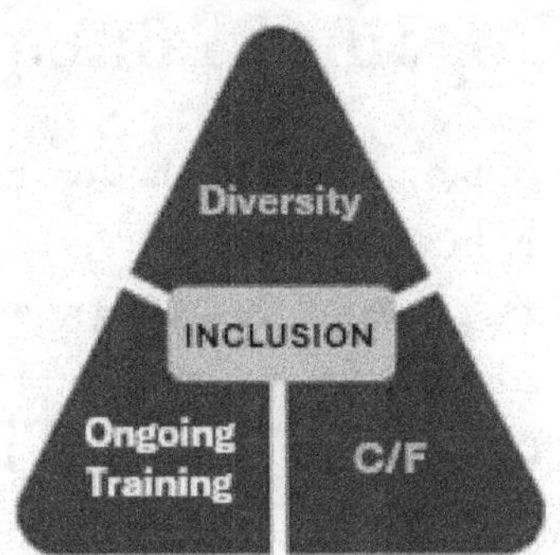
Diversity
INCLUSION
Ongoing
Training
C/F

Ongoing Training

Ongoing training for employees is essential for maintaining a dynamic and effective workplace. In today's rapidly evolving work environment, continuous learning helps employees stay current with the latest industry trends, technological advancements, and best practices. This ongoing education ensures that employees are equipped with up-to-date knowledge and skills, which can enhance their performance and productivity. Moreover, staying informed about new developments allows employees to adapt quickly to changes, contribute innovative ideas, and maintain a competitive edge in the marketplace. Regular training also helps to bridge skill gaps and keep the workforce agile and capable of handling emerging challenges.

Another critical aspect of ongoing training is its role in fostering a culture of continuous improvement and professional growth. When organizations invest in their employees' development, it signals a commitment to their long-term success and career advancement. This not only boosts employee morale but also increases engagement and retention. Employees who see opportunities for growth and development are more likely to stay with the company, feeling valued and motivated to contribute their best efforts. Additionally, fostering a learning culture encourages employees to seek out and embrace new challenges, ultimately driving personal and organizational growth.

Moreover, ongoing training is crucial for addressing evolving issues related to diversity, equity, and inclusion (DEI) and ensuring compliance with regulations and company policies. Regular DEI training helps employees understand and navigate issues related to unconscious bias, harassment, and inclusion, creating a more respectful and equitable workplace. Additionally, compliance training ensures that employees are aware of and adhere to relevant laws and regulations, reducing the risk of legal issues and maintaining organizational integrity. By incorporating ongoing training into the workplace, organizations can promote a positive, informed, and compliant environment that supports both employee well-being and organizational success.

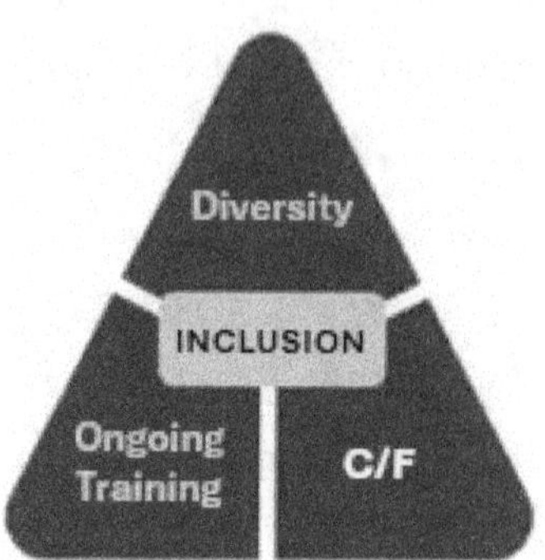

Diversity
INCLUSION
Ongoing
Training
C/F

Communication/Feedback

Open communication and feedback mechanisms are vital for fostering a transparent and collaborative workplace environment. When employees feel that they can freely share their thoughts, concerns, and ideas, it enhances overall engagement and trust within the organization. Open communication channels encourage the exchange of valuable information, which can lead to more effective problem-solving and decision-making. This transparency not only helps in addressing issues before they escalate but also ensures that employees feel heard and valued, creating a more inclusive and supportive workplace culture.

Feedback mechanisms are equally important for continuous improvement and professional growth. Regular and constructive feedback helps employees understand their strengths and areas for development, which can guide their efforts and boost their performance. It provides employees with clear expectations and helps them align their work with organizational goals. Additionally, a structured feedback process allows for the identification of potential issues or areas for enhancement within the team or organization, enabling timely interventions and adjustments. This ongoing dialogue between employees and management promotes a culture of continuous learning and development.

Moreover, having effective communication and feedback systems contributes to resolving conflicts and improving team dynamics. Open communication allows employees to address concerns or misunderstandings directly and constructively, preventing conflicts from escalating. Feedback mechanisms enable management to gauge employee satisfaction and morale, addressing any issues that may affect team cohesion or productivity. By fostering an environment where feedback is regularly exchanged and valued, organizations can build stronger relationships among team members, enhance collaboration, and drive overall organizational success.

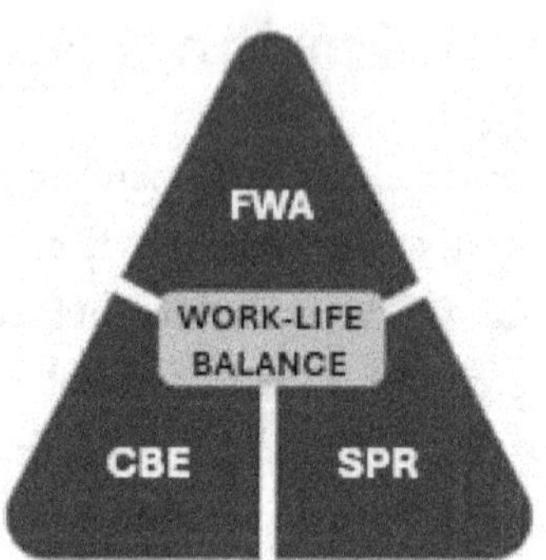
FWA
WORK-LIFE
BALANCE
CBE
SPR

WORK-LIFE BALANCE

Maintaining work-life balance at the workplace requires a multifaceted approach that addresses both organizational practices and individual needs. Here are three key things necessary for achieving this balance:

1. **Flexible Work Arrangements**: Offering flexible work arrangements is essential for helping employees manage their professional and personal responsibilities effectively. This can include options such as flexible working hours, remote work, or hybrid work models. By allowing employees to adjust their schedules or work from different locations, organizations can accommodate diverse needs and personal commitments. Flexibility helps employees better manage their time, reduce stress, and increase overall job satisfaction, leading to improved productivity and well-being.

2. **Clear Boundaries and Expectations**: Establishing clear boundaries and expectations around work and personal time is crucial for maintaining a healthy work-life balance. Organizations should encourage employees to set and respect boundaries, such as avoiding work outside of designated hours or taking regular breaks throughout the day. Clear communication regarding workload expectations and deadlines helps prevent overwork and burnout. By fostering a culture that respects personal time and discourages the expectation of constant availability, organizations support employees in maintaining a more balanced and fulfilling life outside of work.

3. **Supportive Policies and Resources**: Implementing supportive policies and providing resources are key to promoting work-life balance. This can include offering benefits such as paid time off, parental leave, and employee assistance programs. Access to

mental health resources and wellness programs also contributes to overall well-being. Additionally, promoting a culture that values work-life balance through management practices and organizational support reinforces the importance of maintaining this balance. By providing these resources and creating an environment that prioritizes employee well-being, organizations help employees manage their work and personal lives more effectively, leading to greater satisfaction and productivity.

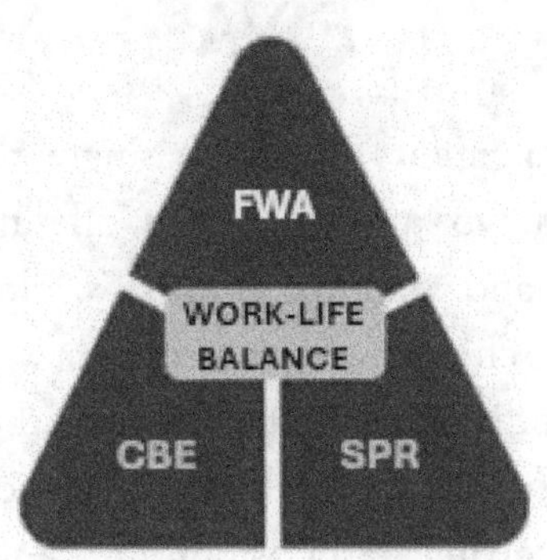

FWA
WORK-LIFE
BALANCE
CBE
SPR

FWA

Flexible work arrangements are increasingly recognized as a vital component of modern workplace practices, offering significant benefits to both employees and organizations. By allowing employees to customize their work schedules or choose their work locations, flexible arrangements help individuals better balance their professional and personal responsibilities. This flexibility is particularly beneficial for employees with caregiving responsibilities, health issues, or other personal commitments, as it enables them to manage their work around their life rather than the other way around. As a result, employees can achieve greater satisfaction and productivity, leading to lower stress levels and enhanced overall well-being.

From an organizational perspective, flexible work arrangements can enhance productivity and employee engagement. When employees have the autonomy to design their work schedules or work remotely, they often experience increased motivation and job satisfaction. This autonomy can lead to higher levels of engagement and creativity, as employees are able to work in ways that best suit their personal productivity patterns and working styles. Additionally, flexible work options can reduce absenteeism and presenteeism, as employees are more likely to stay committed and less likely to take unscheduled leave when they have the ability to adjust their work environment to meet their needs.

Moreover, offering flexible work arrangements can be a powerful tool for attracting and retaining top talent. In today's competitive job market, prospective employees are increasingly looking for workplaces that offer flexibility as a key benefit. Organizations that provide flexible work options are viewed as more progressive and employee-centric, which can enhance their reputation and appeal to high-quality candidates. By accommodating diverse needs and preferences, companies not only improve their employee retention rates but also foster a more inclusive and adaptable workplace culture. This strategic approach to work arrangements helps organizations stay competitive and responsive in an ever-changing business environment.

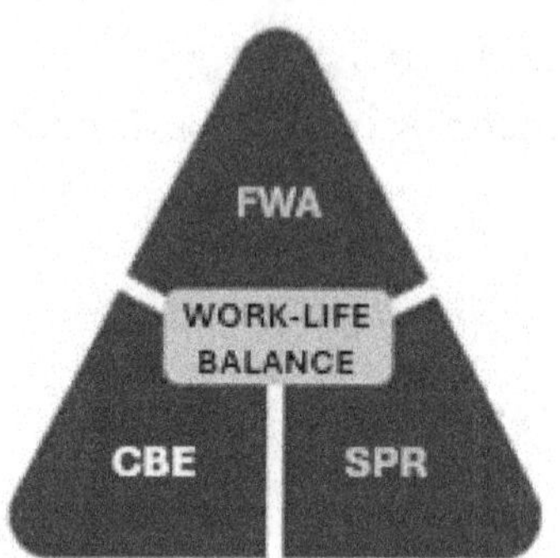

FWA
WORK-LIFE
BALANCE
CBE
SPR

CBE

Establishing **clear boundaries and expectations** in the workplace is crucial for maintaining productivity and employee well-being. Clearly defined boundaries help employees understand their roles, responsibilities, and the limits of their work hours, which can prevent overwork and burnout. When expectations are communicated effectively, employees know what is required of them and can manage their time and efforts accordingly. This clarity helps in setting realistic goals, prioritizing tasks, and maintaining focus, ultimately leading to more efficient work processes and higher quality outcomes.

Also, clear boundaries and expectations foster a healthier work-life balance. By delineating work hours and respecting personal time, organizations create an environment where employees can fully disengage from work when off-duty, reducing stress and improving overall job satisfaction. Establishing guidelines around communication, such as setting limits on after-hours emails or meetings, helps employees manage their personal time effectively. This balance is crucial for preventing burnout and ensuring that employees have the opportunity to rest and recharge, which contributes to sustained productivity and a more positive work environment.

Clear boundaries also play a vital role in preventing conflicts and misunderstandings. When roles and responsibilities are well-defined, it minimizes overlap and confusion, which can lead to disputes and inefficiencies. Employees are less likely to encroach on each other's responsibilities or feel that their work is being undermined. Effective communication of expectations ensures that everyone is aligned and understands their individual contributions to the team's goals. This alignment fosters a collaborative and harmonious workplace where employees can work together effectively and address issues constructively when they arise.

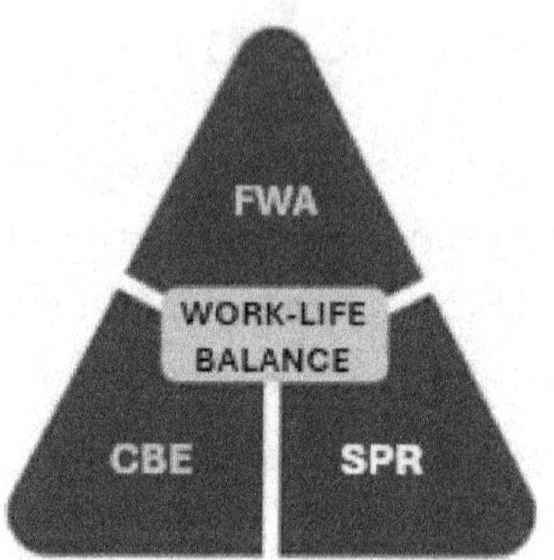
FWA
WORK-LIFE
BALANCE
CBE
SPR

SPR

Supportive policies and resources in the workplace are fundamental to fostering a positive and productive environment where employees can thrive. Policies such as paid time off, parental leave, and flexible working arrangements provide employees with the support they need to manage their personal and professional lives effectively. These policies demonstrate the organization's commitment to employee well-being and contribute to a more balanced and fulfilling work experience. By offering these benefits, companies not only enhance job satisfaction and retention but also create a more inclusive workplace that accommodates diverse needs and life circumstances.

In addition to formal policies, providing resources such as employee assistance programs, wellness initiatives, and professional development opportunities is crucial for supporting employees. Employee assistance programs offer confidential counseling and support for personal issues, helping employees manage stress and maintain mental health. Wellness initiatives, including health screenings, fitness programs, and mental health resources, promote overall well-being and prevent burnout. Investing in professional development opportunities, such as training and education, helps employees advance their skills and career prospects, contributing to their long-term success and satisfaction. These resources create a supportive environment that enables employees to perform at their best and grow both personally and professionally.

Supportive policies and resources also play a critical role in enhancing organizational resilience and adaptability. By addressing the diverse needs of employees and providing tools to manage challenges, organizations can build a more engaged and loyal workforce. When employees feel supported and valued, they are more likely to contribute positively to the organization and adapt to changes with greater ease. This support helps maintain high levels of productivity and morale, even during times of stress or transition. Ultimately, having well-designed policies and resources in place strengthens the organization's ability to retain top talent, navigate challenges effectively, and achieve long-term success.

Training
SAFETY
Equipment
Report/
Response
Diversity
WORK
PLACE
FWA
INCLUSION
WORK-LIFE
BALANCE
Ongoing
Training
C/F
CBE
SPR

SUMMARY

Employees have several key expectations from the workplace they are employed at, which play a significant role in their overall job satisfaction and productivity. First and foremost, employees expect fair and equitable treatment. This includes a commitment to diversity and inclusion, where every individual is valued and given equal opportunities for advancement regardless of their background. Employees also anticipate transparent and consistent application of company policies, ensuring that promotions, rewards, and disciplinary actions are based on merit and are applied impartially. Fair treatment builds trust and motivates employees to contribute their best efforts to the organization.

Another critical expectation is for clear and open communication. Employees expect to be kept informed about organizational changes, their performance, and their roles and responsibilities. This includes receiving constructive feedback that helps them improve and grow professionally. Effective communication also involves having accessible channels for expressing concerns, suggestions, or grievances, ensuring that their voices are heard and addressed. Transparent and regular communication fosters a collaborative environment, reduces misunderstandings, and aligns employees with the organization's goals and values.

Lastly, employees expect a supportive and resourceful work environment that prioritizes their well-being and professional development. This includes having access to necessary tools, training, and resources that enable them to perform their jobs effectively and advance their skills. Employees also seek a healthy work-life balance, supported by policies that allow them to manage their personal and professional responsibilities without undue stress. A workplace that invests in employee development, well-being, and work-life balance not only enhances job satisfaction but also boosts engagement and retention, contributing to the overall success of the organization.

Invitation

In my 50+ years of working, I have been an employee, a consultant, an employer and a business owner. It's safe to say, I have been on both sides of the fence when it comes to the workplace.

When you get right down to it, employers use their employees to get where they want to go with the business. Conversely, employees used their employers to achieve things on their own agenda as well. That said, employers are not emotionally attached to employees typically. Nor are employees emotionally attached to their employers.

Back in our grandparents and parents' generation, company/ employee loyalty meant something. Both my grandfather and father were lifelong employees of the same company. My mother worked at her employment for 25 years. The older generation picked one employer, one spouse, one house, one car and one church. They stuck with them until the end of their retirement and lives, for the most part. Those days are long gone!

In today's world, it's basically every man/woman for themselves. There is no loyalty either way due to different dynamics today. Everyone understands that and does what they can to protect their best interests.

So, I said all of that, to say this: our expectations of others should not be very high. Things can change on a dime with cyclical economy or supply and demand. Also, private equity firms are buying and selling companies all day long. It would be nice if loyalty was like it used to be but alas, that's not the case.

It's nothing personal, it's just the way things are. "What's mine is mine and what's yours is yours. You stay on your side of the fence, and I'll stay on mine." seems to be the attitude of the 21st century.

If you're lucky to be at a great workplace, then embrace it. If not, move on until you find the right fit. We spend too much time at work not to enjoy it.

Quotes on the Workplace

1. "The strength of the team is each individual member. The strength of each member is the team."
   — Phil Jackson

1. "To handle yourself, use your head; to handle others, use your heart."
   — Eleanor Roosevelt

1. "Work is not just about what you do but how you do it and who you do it with."
   — Unknown

1. "The only way to do great work is to love what you do."
   — Steve Jobs

1. "A good leader is one who knows the way, goes the way, and shows the way."
   — John C. Maxwell

1. "Culture eats strategy for breakfast."
   — Peter Drucker

1. "Employees who believe that management is concerned about them as a whole person—not just an employee—are more productive, more satisfied, more fulfilled."
   — Anne M. Mulcahy

1. "The best way to predict the future is to create it."
   — Peter Drucker
2. "In a team, there is no 'I' but there is a 'we.'"
   — Unknown

1. "Success is not the key to happiness. Happiness is the key to success. If you love what you are doing, you will be successful."
    — Albert Schweitzer

Here is a list of fundamental **employee rights** typically upheld in the workplace:

1. **Right to Fair Compensation**: Employees have the right to receive fair and timely wages for their work, including overtime pay where applicable. This encompasses compliance with minimum wage laws and any contractual agreements regarding compensation.

2. **Right to a Safe Work Environment**: Employees are entitled to a workplace that is free from hazards and complies with occupational health and safety regulations. Employers must ensure that safety protocols are followed and provide necessary training and equipment.

3. **Right to Non-Discrimination**: Employees should not be discriminated against based on race, gender, age, disability, religion, sexual orientation, or any other protected characteristic. Equal treatment in hiring, promotions, and job assignments is mandated.

4. **Right to Privacy**: Employees have a right to privacy concerning their personal information and activities. Employers must handle personal data with confidentiality and respect privacy boundaries, including limitations on workplace surveillance and personal searches.

5. **Right to Freedom from Harassment**: Employees have the right to work in an environment free from harassment, including sexual harassment, bullying, and any form of abusive behavior. Employers are responsible for enforcing anti-harassment policies and addressing complaints promptly.

6. **Right to Fair Treatment**: Employees should be treated fairly and equitably, with transparent processes for performance evaluations, promotions, and disciplinary actions. They have the right to appeal decisions that they believe are unjust.

7. **Right to Join a Union**: Employees have the right to join or

form a union and to engage in collective bargaining without fear of retaliation. Union membership should not affect employment status or job security.

8. **Right to Reasonable Accommodations**: Employees with disabilities or specific needs are entitled to reasonable accommodations that enable them to perform their job duties effectively, provided this does not cause undue hardship to the employer.

9. **Right to Leave and Time Off**: Employees have the right to take leave for various reasons, such as personal illness, family emergencies, or parental leave, in accordance with applicable laws and company policies.

10. **Right to Health Benefits**: In many jurisdictions, employees are entitled to health benefits, including access to medical insurance or other health-related benefits, as stipulated by employment agreements or legal requirements.

These rights help ensure a fair, respectful, and legally compliant workplace, contributing to overall employee satisfaction and organizational effectiveness.

Employers also have specific **rights** in the workplace to ensure effective management and operational efficiency. Here's a list of key employer rights:

1. **Right to Set Job Requirements and Performance Standards**: Employers have the right to establish job descriptions, performance expectations, and requirements for positions within their organization. This includes setting goals and standards for employee performance and evaluating their work against these benchmarks.

2. **Right to Manage and Direct Work**: Employers have the authority to direct the work of their employees, including assigning tasks, setting work schedules, and making decisions regarding job responsibilities. This right ensures that the organization's objectives are met and operations run smoothly.

3. **Right to Enforce Workplace Policies**: Employers have the right to implement and enforce workplace policies, such as codes of conduct, attendance requirements, and safety protocols. This includes taking disciplinary action when policies are violated to maintain order and compliance.

4. **Right to Privacy of Business Operations**: Employers have the right to protect the confidentiality of their business operations, including proprietary information, trade secrets, and internal communications. This right ensures that sensitive business information is not disclosed improperly.

5. **Right to Evaluate Employee Performance**: Employers are entitled to conduct performance evaluations and assessments to ensure employees meet the required standards and contribute effectively to the organization. This includes providing feedback and setting objectives for performance improvement.

6. **Right to Hire and Terminate Employees**: Employers have the authority to make decisions about hiring, promoting, and

terminating employees based on their business needs and performance. This right allows employers to build a team that aligns with the company's goals and requirements.

7. **Right to Request and Verify Employee Information**: Employers have the right to request necessary information from employees for the purpose of verifying qualifications, conducting background checks, and ensuring eligibility for employment. This includes verifying credentials and work history.

8. **Right to Establish Compensation and Benefits**: Employers have the right to determine compensation structures, including salaries, wages, and benefits packages. This includes setting pay rates and designing benefits programs that align with the organization's compensation strategy.

9. **Right to Discipline Employees**: Employers have the authority to take disciplinary actions, including warnings, suspensions, or termination, for breaches of conduct or performance issues. This right is essential for maintaining a productive and compliant work environment.

10. **Right to Create and Implement Business Strategies**: Employers have the right to develop and implement business strategies and operational plans to achieve organizational goals. This includes making decisions about company direction, market positioning, and resource allocation.

These rights enable employers to effectively manage their organizations, maintain operational efficiency, and ensure that business objectives are met while balancing the needs and rights of employees.

When someone is struggling with a particular area or two, chances are they are "out of balance" with how life works. How does life work? Life works in threes.

If you're interested in personal topics like life, health, money or business topics like sales, time management and public speaking...Life Works in Threes! can shed some light on creating success in those areas.

The definition of TRIUNE is a group of three things; united. Being three in one, such as - humans are *mental, physical* and *spiritual beings.* The word TRYUNE is a play of the word TRIUNE, encouraging all to try this concept and help eliminate struggling unnecessarily.

LifeWorksInThrees.com

www.ingramcontent.com/pod-product-compliance
Lightning Source LLC
Chambersburg PA
CBHW052226150726
48002CB00003B/1291